NATIONAL GEOGRAPHIC Little kids™

WORD BOOK

LEARNING THE WORDS IN YOUR WORLD

seashell

apple

Jim Bear

tiger

steamroller

NATIONAL GEOGRAPHIC

WASHINGTON, D.C.

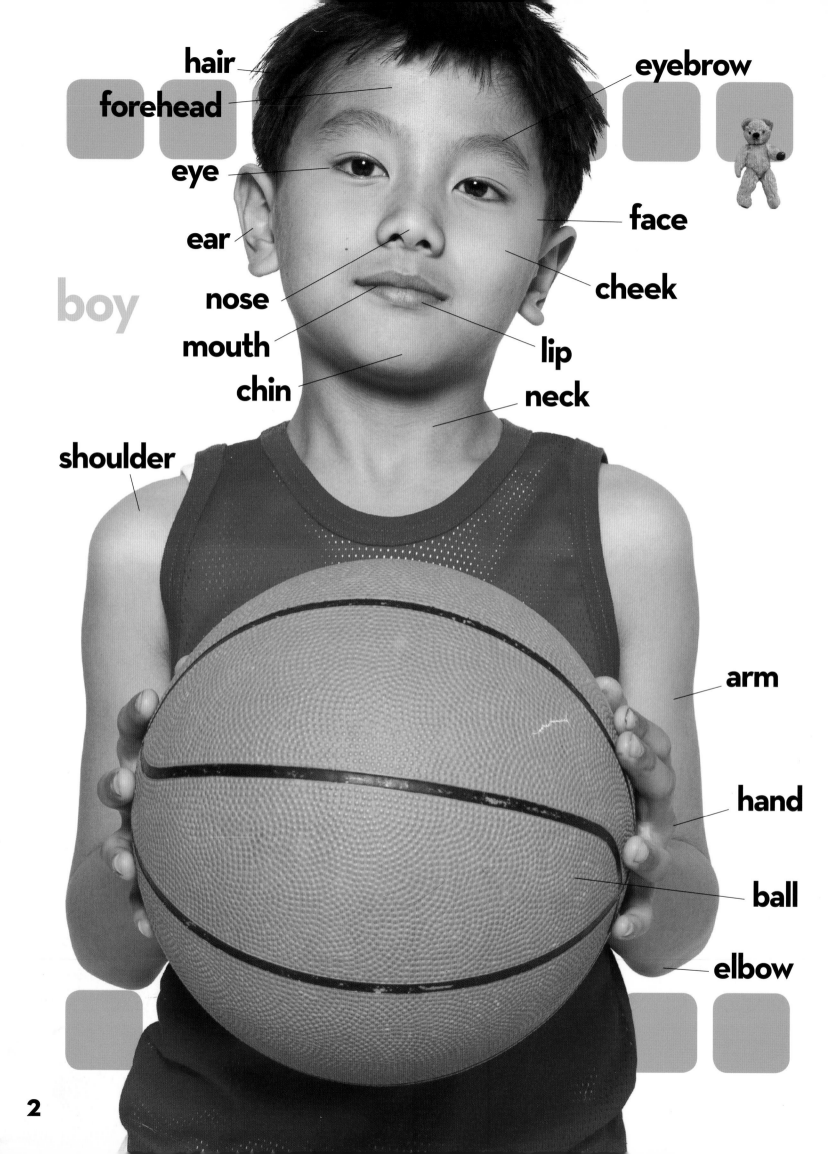

hair

eyebrow

forehead

eye

face

ear

cheek

boy

nose

mouth

lip

chin

neck

shoulder

arm

hand

ball

elbow

2

CONTENTS

How to Use This Book 4
Alphabet Letters 6
Numbers 8
Shapes 10
Patterns 11
Colors 12
Car 14
Body 16
Clothes 17
The House 18
The Garden 20
Good Morning 22
Good Night 23
What We Eat and Drink 24
Family and Friends 26
School 27
Fun and Games 28
In the Street 30
In the Kitchen 32
Fruit 34
Vegetables 35
Baby Animals 36
Pets 37

By the Sea 38
On the Farm 40
Party Time 42
Let's Make Music 44
Wild Animals 46
On the Move! 48
Creepy Crawlies 50
I Am Big! 52
Shopping 54
In the Workshop 56
Out and About 58
Weather 60
Seasons 61
Time 62
Index 63

Betty Bear

HOW TO USE THIS BOOK

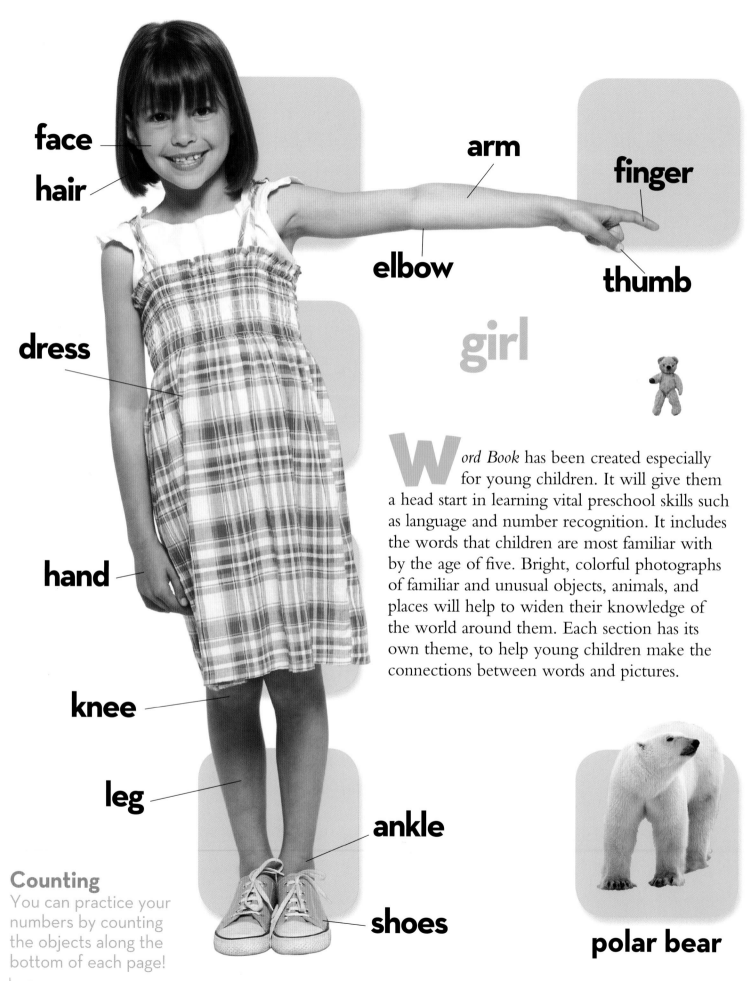

What pattern is the girl's **dress**?

What color is the **polar bear**?

face

hair

arm

finger

elbow

thumb

girl

dress

hand

knee

leg

ankle

shoes

polar bear

Word Book has been created especially for young children. It will give them a head start in learning vital preschool skills such as language and number recognition. It includes the words that children are most familiar with by the age of five. Bright, colorful photographs of familiar and unusual objects, animals, and places will help to widen their knowledge of the world around them. Each section has its own theme, to help young children make the connections between words and pictures.

Counting
You can practice your numbers by counting the objects along the bottom of each page!

4

Young children like to look at pictures and love naming what they see. It is even more fun for them to share a word book with an adult. Start by talking about what is in the picture, and what the object might be used for. Talk about colors and shapes. Look at the scale of the objects—they might be very different on different pages. You can use the questions around the edges of the pages to start a conversation and encourage the child to study the pictures more closely. When they are familiar with the book, show them the index in the back, and explain how it is organized alphabetically.

A Note for Kids
Jim and Betty Bear are hidden on each page of this book. Look closely and see if you can spot them. How many did you count?

(see answer on page 64)

hair

eyebrow

eye

nose

Betty Bear

Jim Bear

boy

shirt

ALPHABET LETTERS

What words can you spell using the alphabet?

Can you read all of your **letters**?

Can you find a **Q** and an **R**?

A a

B b

C c

D d

E e

F f

G g

H h

I i

J j

K k

L l

M m

A A A A A A

How many letters are in the alphabet?

N n

O o

P p

Q q

R r

S s

T t

U u

V v

W w

X x

Y y

Z z

NUMBERS

Can you count all the way to 32?

one

two

three

four

five

six

seven

eight

nine

ten

eleven

twelve

thirteen

fourteen

fifteen

sixteen

Can you point to **10** and **20**?

Can you count to **30**?

8

Can you point to all the numbers after 12?

seventeen

eighteen

nineteen

twenty

twenty-one

twenty-two

twenty-three

twenty-four

twenty-five

twenty-six

twenty-seven

twenty-eight

twenty-nine

thirty

thirty-one

thirty-two

■ Which number comes after **19**?

■ Can you point to number **21**?

SHAPES

Can you draw these shapes?

square

pentagon

right triangle

cylinder

hexagon

cone

rectangle

cube

sphere

octagon

circle

oval

star

heart

PATTERNS

What patterns are the bears wearing?

spots

plaid

checks

zigzag

wavy

stars

stripes

COLORS

Which color do you like best?

red   orange   yellow   green   blue

paintbox   blue

silver

pen

urple　pink　brown　gray　black

white

brushes

yellow　red

gold

CAR

Are the headlights at the front or back of the car?

What shape are the **wheels**?

Where is the **hood**?

seat

roof

rear window

taillight

back

bumper

wheel

door handle

Can you find the **lights**?

Where is the door **handle**?

steering wheel

side-view mirror

windshield

hood

What color is the **car**?

front

door

headlight

BODY

face

hair

eyebrow

eye

nose

cheek

ear

mouth

teeth

lip

chin

neck

arm

hand

head

elbow

chest

tummy

hip

leg

knee

feet

CLOTHES

Which boys have shirts with stripes?

shirt

pajamas

socks

slippers

hat

dress

shoes

school uniform

shorts

shirt

hat

bag

jeans

sweat-shirt

sneakers

 What color is the **shirt**?

What do you wear to **bed**?

What color is the boy's **hat**?

THE HOUSE

Can you find these objects in your own home?

What color is the **telephone**? ● What time is it on the **clock**? ● Can you see a **cat**?

armchair

rug

phone

end table

bookcase

book

cushion

computer

clock

sofa

chimney　　**roof**　　**window**

wall　　**door**　　**garage**　　**gate**

radio　　**flowers**　　**keys**　　**newspapers**

frames　　**television**　　**MP3 player**

THE GARDEN

Which object would you use to water plants?

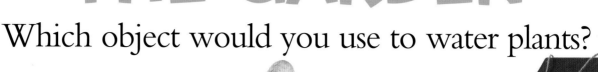

What color is the **rose**?

How many prongs are on the **garden fork**?

rake

garden fork

rose

birdhouse

shears

flowerpot

watering can

bonfire

wheelbarrow

trowel

rubber boots

■ Can you point to the **birdhouse**?　　■ Where is the **tree house**?

bush　　**sky**　　**tree**　　**tree house**

flowers　　**bench**　　**hedge**　　**grass**

■ Can you find a **rake?**　　■ What color is the **wheelbarrow?**

GOOD MORNING

What time do you wake up?

What color is the **washcloth**?

What color is the **quilt**?

sun

washcloth

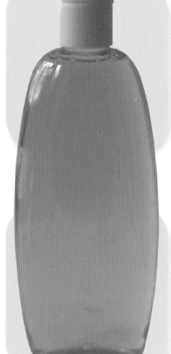

shampoo

toilet paper

**brushing
your teeth**

soap

toothbrush

toothpaste

22

GOOD NIGHT

When do you go to bed?

bed

toilet

teddy

girl

pajamas

pillows

quilt

sleepover

moon

book

sleep

slippers

■ Where is the **moon**?

■ Can you find the **soap**?

■ What pattern is on the **pillows**?

    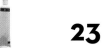

WHAT WE EAT AND DRINK

Which is your favorite **food**?

Can you see the **turkey**?

Where is the **pizza**?

milk

rice

cheese

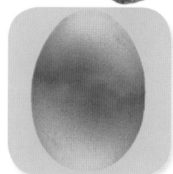

egg

doughnut

cookies

tacos

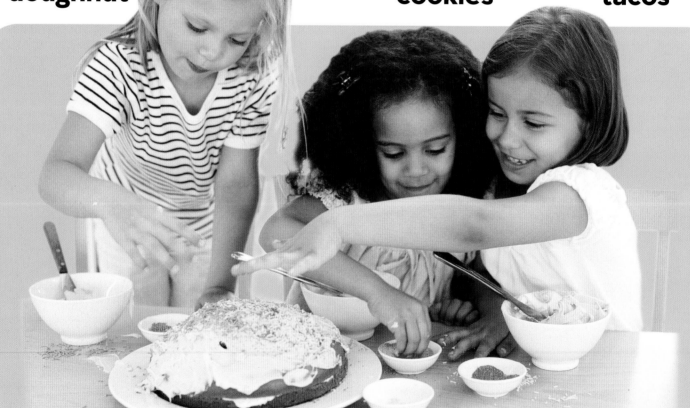

cake

sweets

bread

strawberries

■ Can you find the **steak**?

steak

scrambled eggs

turkey

salad

hot dog

■ What color is the **cheese**?

seafood

pizza

pancake

burger

FAMILY AND FRIENDS

How many people are in your family?

Can you see a **mother**?

Can you see a group of **friends**?

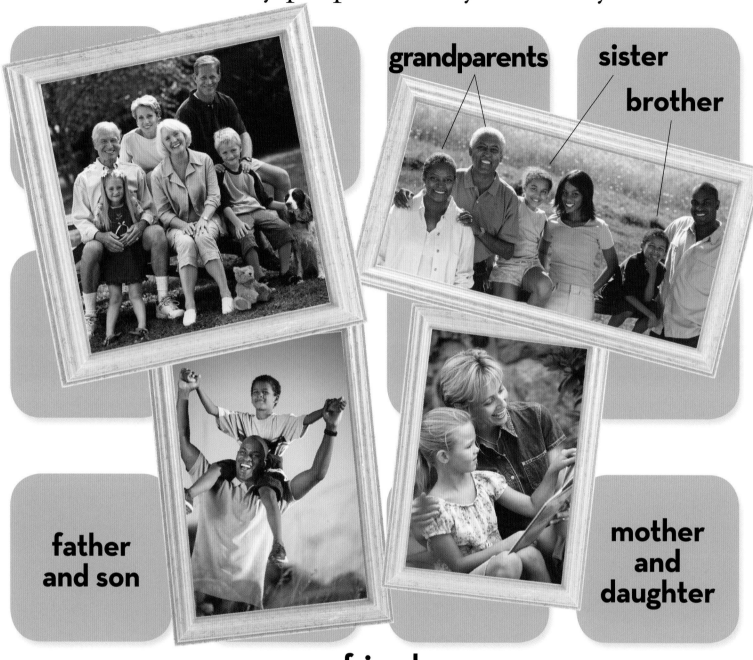

grandparents

sister

brother

father and son

mother and daughter

friends

SCHOOL

What subjects do you study at school?

What colors can you **see**?

Can you find the **scissors**?

markers

protractor

paint

triangle

computer

pencils

ruler

notebook

scissors

FUN AND GAMES

What is your favorite game?

Can you find some **cards**?

Can you find things that **bounce**?

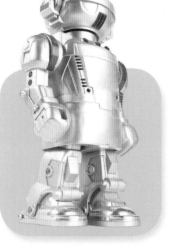

robot

soccer ball

drawing

puppet

basketball

cards

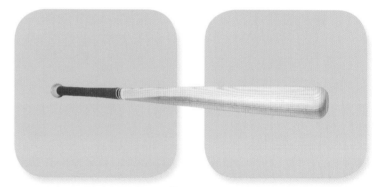

bat

wooden blocks

painting

jump rope

climbing

model plane

jungle gym

28

What sports do you like?

chess

bubbles

tricycle

balloon

playing soccer

jumping

playing with dolls

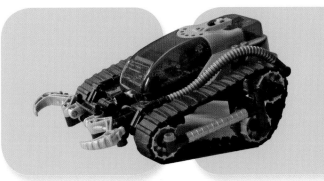

robot car

stuffed animals

29

IN THE STREET

What can you find on your street?

Can you see the **gate**?

Where are the **police**?

street lamp

fire hydrant

speed camera

phone booth

trash can

gate

police

statue

construction site

recycling bin

traffic light

firemen

atm

30

■ Where are the **firemen**?　　■ What color is the **trash can**?

street lamp　　**tower**　　**bridge**　　**window**

sidewalk　　**car**　　**pole**　　**building**

■ Can you find the telephone **booth**?　　■ What colors is the **traffic light**?

IN THE KITCHEN

What do you use to stir things?

Can you point to the **whisk**?

canned food

pitcher

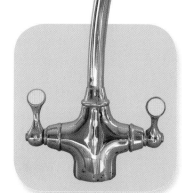

washing machine

faucet

egg cup

toaster

bowl

dish towel

refrigerator

teapot

saucepan

cereal

32

What can run hot and cold?

knife and fork

teacup

frying pan

whisk

oven

iron

ice cream scoop

plates

kettle

● What color is the **teapot**?

● Can you find a **bowl**?

FRUIT

Can you point to the pineapple?

Can you see a **pepper**?

Where is the **orange**?

Can you find a **watermelon**?

bananas

apple

pineapple

lime

pear

grapes

kiwi

lemon

grapefruit

watermelon

peach

orange

tomato

strawberry

cherry

VEGETABLES

Can you find a turnip?

cauliflower

onion

broccoli

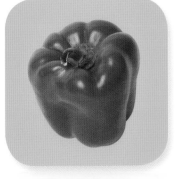
mushroom

turnip

potatoes

celery

pepper

string beans

corn

carrots

radishes

lettuce

● Where is the **mushroom**? ● Can you see the **potatoes**? ● Can you see a **pear**?

BABY ANIMALS

What is a baby horse called?

What is a **baby dog** called?

Can you find the **bear cub**?

Where is the **fawn**?

kittens

ducklings

foal

calf

piglet

chicks

fawn

puppy

cygnet

lamb

cub

36

PETS

Do you have any pets?

rabbit

dog

guinea pig

washing the dog

fish

cat

parrot

tortoise

Does a **tortoise** move fast or slow? ● Which pet can **fly**? ● Can you find a **cat**?

BY THE SEA

What do you use to see underwater?

beach ball

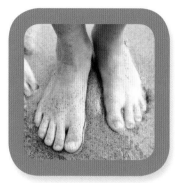
wading

bucket

lighthouse

mask

waves

flippers

inflatable tubes

pinwheel

swimming

beach chair

38

What can you **dig** with?

What letter and number can you see on the **fishing boat**?

shell

crab

surfer

fishing boat

beach

sunglasses

What can you **sit on**?

39

ON THE FARM

How many animals have two legs?

How many **tractors** can you find?

turkey

duck

donkey

wheat

corn

hen

plowing a field

pig

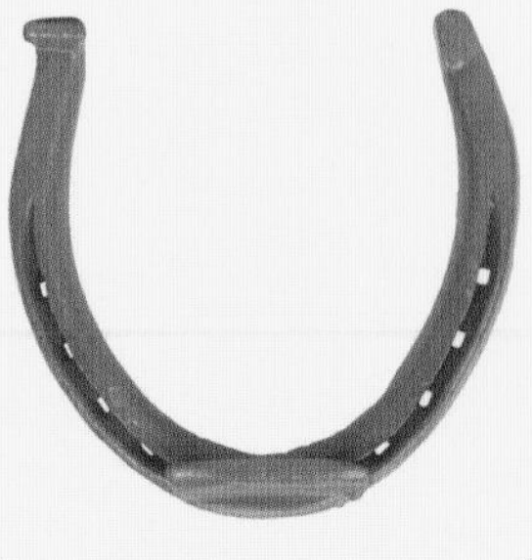

horseshoe

pony

cow

What color is the rooster's tail?

hay bale

sheep

barn

tractor

rooster

goose

horses

goat

butter churn

PARTY TIME

What colors are the balloons?

balloons

sandwiches

silver bow

party hat

card

ribbons

gift tag

birthday cake

candle

Can you find four hats?

presents

ice cream

clown

tart

fruit salad

wrapping paper

Mr. T Bear Esq
6 Bear House
Bearsville-Upon-Sea
BEARTUCKY
ABC 123

juice

envelope

face paint

LET'S MAKE MUSIC

Which instrument has black and white keys?

Where are the **bongos**? ● Can you find a **triangle**? ● Can you see the **viola**?

flute and recorder

tambourine

saxophone

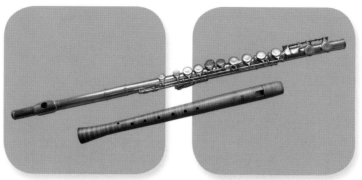

piano

guitar

banjo

microphone

bongos

triangle

violin

bugle

French horn

How many instruments have strings?

bagpipes　　**drum**　　**viola**　　**trombone**

■How many **drums** can you find?

musicians

■Can you spot the **guitar**?

45

WILD ANIMALS

How many animals have feathers?

panda

crocodile

swan

shark

wolf

cheetah

reindeer

crab

penguin

polar bear

hare

zebra

gorilla

Can you see the crocodile?

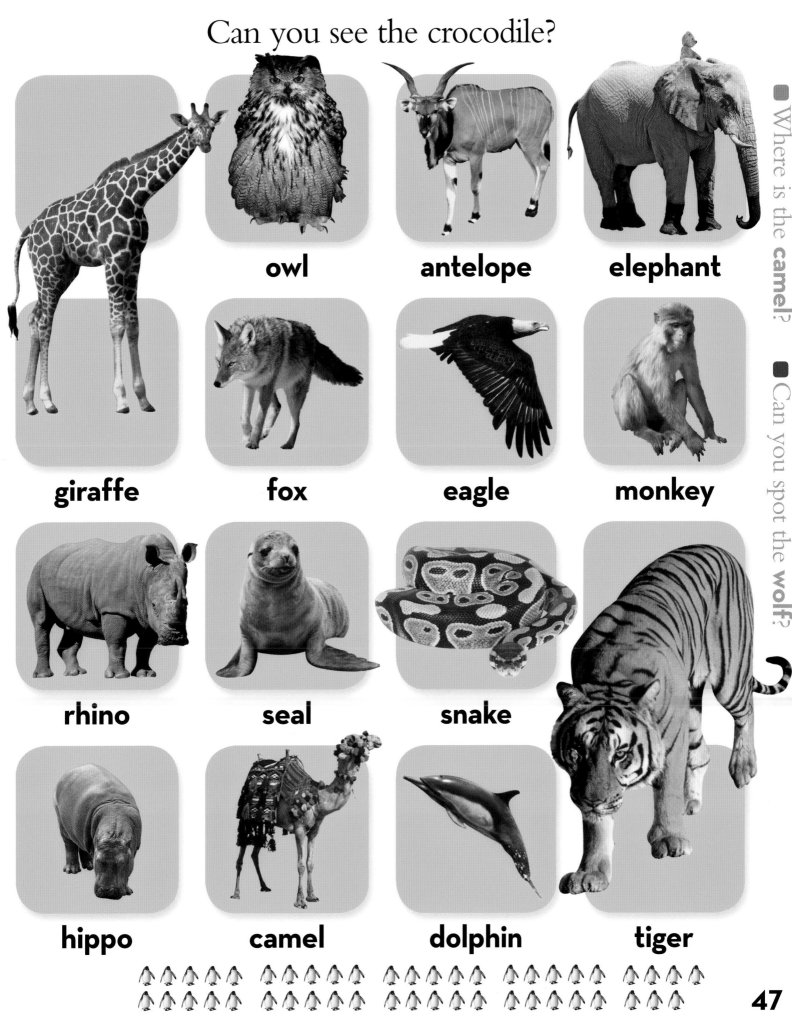

owl

antelope

elephant

giraffe

fox

eagle

monkey

rhino

seal

snake

hippo

camel

dolphin

tiger

■ Where is the **camel**?   ■ Can you spot the **wolf**?

47

ON THE MOVE!

Which of these vehicles can travel on water?

Can you see the **space shuttle**?

train

hot air balloon

boat

Can you see the **plane**?

cruise ship

skateboard

motorcycle

What color is the **car**?

watercraft

hovercraft

plane

snowmobile

raft

Which vehicle travels on snow?

space shuttle

truck

bus

streetcar

bicycle

scooter

car

helicopter

CREEPY CRAWLIES

How many ants can you spot?

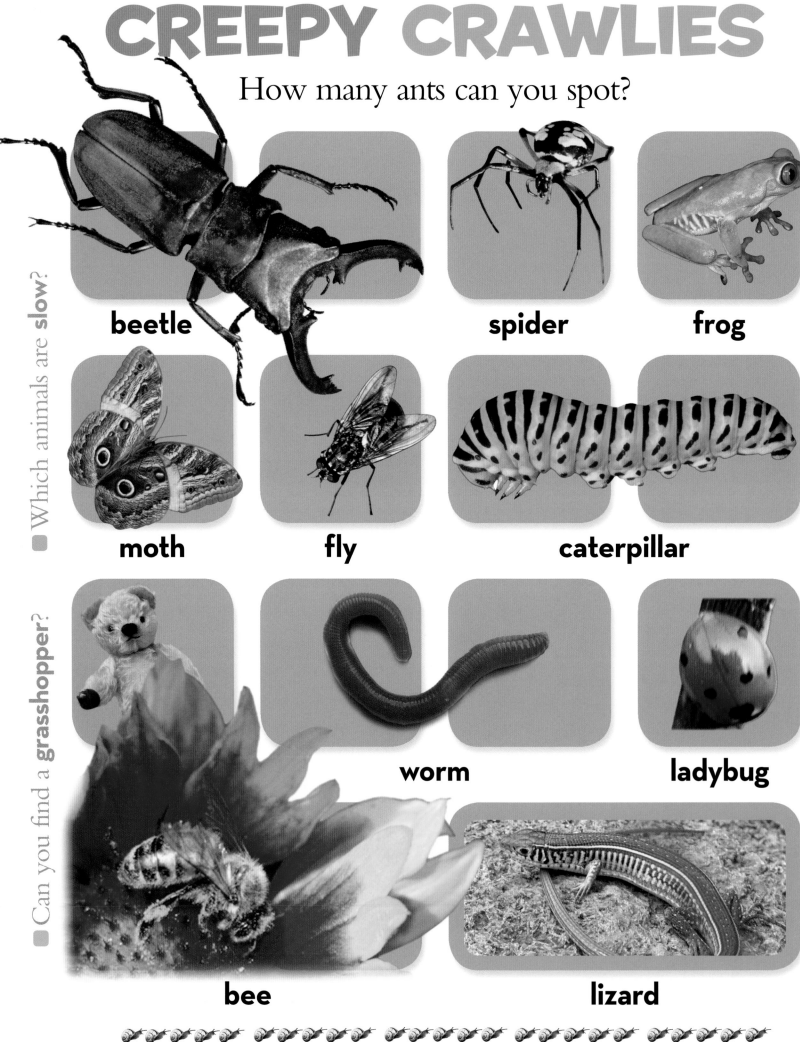

beetle

spider

frog

Which animals are **slow**?

moth

fly

caterpillar

Can you find a **grasshopper**?

worm

ladybug

bee

lizard

Where are the two different spiders?

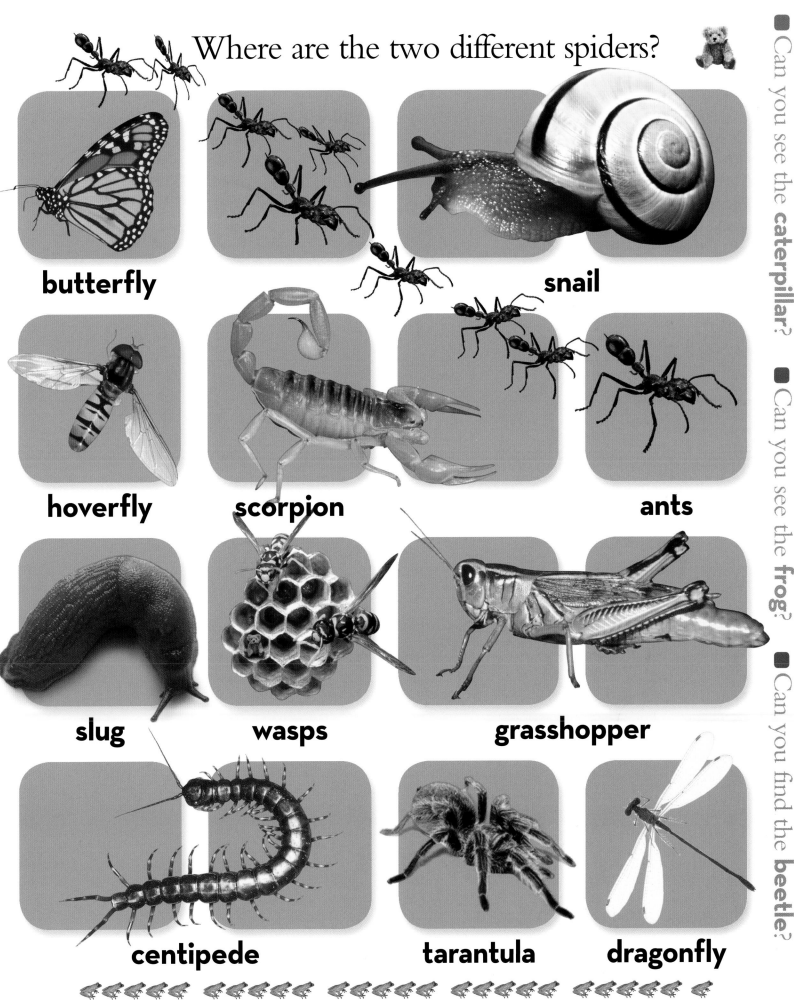

butterfly

snail

hoverfly   **scorpion**

ants

slug   **wasps**

grasshopper

centipede

tarantula

dragonfly

I AM BIG!

Where is the **cargo ship**?

Can you see an **iceberg**?

Where is the **tree**?

logging machine

crane

steamroller

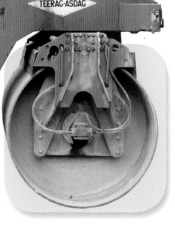

rocket

whale

tree

What has **big ears**?   Can you see the **bison**?

Where is the logging machine?

castle

bison

cargo ship

elephant

airplane

iceberg

bulldozer

Can you point to the **rocket**?   Can you find the **steamroller**?

SHOPPING

How many men are getting haircuts?

bakery

candy store

grocery store

craft store

delicatessen

barbershop

fabric store

fish market

butcher shop

flower shop

toy store

music store

dress shop

Where can you buy **fish?** ● Where can you find the **craft store?** ● Can you find the **craft store?** ● Where can you buy **flowers?** ● Where can you buy

How many carrots do you see?

■ Can you point to the **green beans**?

■ Can you spot the **radishes**?

farmers market

IN THE WORKSHOP

What color is the oil can?

Can you find the **hammer**?

Where is the **vise**?

Where is the **paintbrush**?

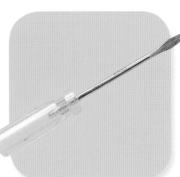

screwdriver

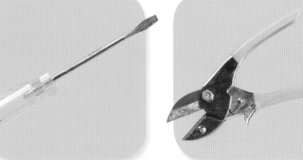

pruner

paintbrush

wrench

pliers

tape measure

oil can

plane

nut and bolt

trowel

workshop

Are there eight wrenches in the set?

set of wrenches

toolbox

axe

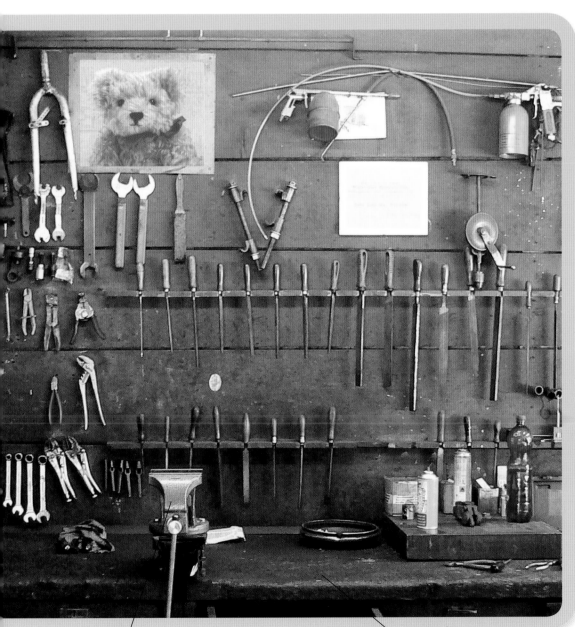

saw

hammer

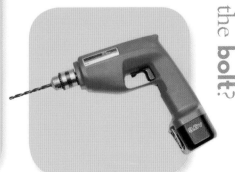

vise　　**bench**　　**electric drill**

OUT AND ABOUT

Where would you go to catch a plane?

Where would you find lots of **buildings**?

mountain

city

Can you find a **bridge**?

waterfall

river   **bridge**

Where would you find lots of boats?

highway

canal

airport

buildings

train station

lake

harbor

WEATHER

Where is the **flood**? ▪ Can you see the **fog**? ▪ Where is the **tornado**?

umbrella

raincoat

snow

hurricane

tornado

lightning

flood

rainbow

fog

SEASONS

Which season follows winter?

spring

summer

fall

winter

● When do the leaves turn **orange?** ■ When does it **snow?** ■ Can you see the **sunflowers?**

TIME

How many hours are there in a day?

nighttime

wake-up time

morning time

breakfast time

bedtime

toothbrush time

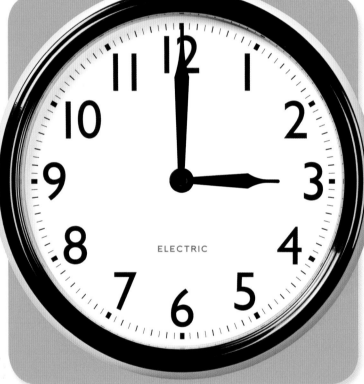

clock

ELECTRIC

school time

lunchtime

dinnertime

playtime

going home time

class time

INDEX

How many words start with the letter E?

A

airplane 53
airport 59
alphabet letters 6–7
animals
  baby 36
  wild 46–47
ankle 4
antelope 47
ants 51
apple 1, 34
arm 2, 4, 16
armchair 18
ATM 30
axe 57

B

baby animals 36
bag 17
bagpipes 45
bakery 54
ball 2
balloon (hot air) 48
balloon (toy) 29, 42
bananas 34
banjo 44
barbershop 54
barn 41
basketball 28
bat 28
beach 39
beach ball 38
beach chair 38
bear 1, 4, 5, 46
  see also teddy
bed 23
bedtime 62
bee 50
beetle 50
bench 21, 57
Betty Bear 3, 5
bicycle 49
big things 52–53
birdhouse 20
birthday cake 42
bison 53
black 13
blue 12
boat 48
body 16
bolt 56
bonfire 20
bongos 44

book 18, 23
bookcase 18
bow 42
bowl 32
boy 2, 5
bread 25
breakfast time 62
bridge 31, 58
broccoli 35
brother 26
brown 13
brushing your teeth 22
bubbles 29
bucket 38
bugle 44
buildings 31, 59
bulldozer 53
bumper 14
burger 25
bus 49
bush 21
butter churn 41
butterfly 51

C

calf 36
camel 47
canal 59
candle 42
candy store 54
canned food 32
car 14–15, 31, 49
cards 28, 42
cargo ship 53
carrots 35
castle 53
cat 37
caterpillar 50
cauliflower 35
celery 35
centipede 51
cereal 32
checks 11
cheek 2, 16
cheese 24
cheetah 46
cherry 34
chess 29
chest 16
chicks 36
chimney 19
chin 2, 16
circle 10
city 58
class time 62
climbing 28
clock 18, 62

clothes 17
clown 43
colors 12–13
computer 18, 27
cone 10
construction site 30
cookies 24
corn 35
cow 40
crab 39, 46
craft store 54
crane 52
creepy crawlies 50–51
crocodile 46
cruise ship 48
cub 36
cube 10
cushion 18
cygnet 36
cylinder 10

D

daughter 26
delicatessen 54
dinnertime 62
dish towel 32
dog 37
dolls 29
dolphin 47
donkey 40
door 15, 19
door handle 14
doughnut 24
dragonfly 51
drawing 28
dress 4, 17
dress shop 54
drum 45
duck 40
ducklings 36

E

eagle 47
ear 2, 16
eating 24
egg cup 32
eggs 24, 25
elbow 2, 4, 16
electric drill 57
elephant 47, 53
envelope 43
eye 2, 5, 16
eyebrow 2, 5, 16

F

fabric store 54
face 2, 4, 16
face paint 43
fall 61
family 26
farm 40–41
farmers market 55
father 26
faucet 32
fawn 36
feet 16
finger 4
fire hydrant 30
firemen 30
fish 37
fishing boat 39
fish market 54
flippers 38
flood 60
flowers 21
flower shop 54
flute 44
fly 50
foal 36
fog 60
forehead 2
fork 33
fox 47
frames 19
French horn 44
friends 26
frog 50
fruit 34
fruit salad 43
frying pan 33
fun 28–29

G

games 28–29
garage 19
garden 20–21
garden fork 20
gate 19, 30
gift tag 42
giraffe 47
girl 4, 23
goat 41
going home time 62
gold 13
goose 41
gorilla 46
grandparents 26
grapefruit 34

grapes 34
grass 21
grasshopper 51
gray 13
green 12
grocery store 54
guinea pig 37
guitar 44

H

hair 2, 4, 5, 16
hammer 57
hand 2, 4, 16
harbor 59
hare 46
hat 17, 42
hay bale 41
head 16
headlight 15
heart 10
hedge 21
helicopter 49
hen 40
hexagon 10
highway 59
hip 16
hippo 47
hood 15
horses 41
horseshoe 40
house 18–19
hovercraft 48
hoverfly 51
hurricane 60

I

iceberg 53
ice cream 43
ice-cream scoop 33
inflatable tubes 38
iron 33

J

jeans 17
Jim Bear 1, 5
juice 43
jumping 29
jump rope 28
jungle gym 28

K

kettle 33
keys 19
kitchen 32–33
kittens 36
kiwi 34
knee 4, 16
knife 33

L

ladybug 50
lake 59
lamb 36
leg 4, 16
lemon 34
lettuce 35
lighthouse 38
lightning 60
lime 34
lip 2, 16
lizard 50
logging machine 52
lunchtime 62

M

markers 27
mask 38
microphone 44
milk 24
model plane 28
monkey 47
moon 23
morning 22, 62
moth 50
mother 26
motorcycle 48
mountain 58
mouth 2, 16
MP3 player 19
mushroom 35
music 44–45
musicians 45
music store 54

N

neck 2, 16
newspapers 19
night 23, 62
nose 2, 5, 16
notebook 27
numbers 8–9
nut 56

O

octagon 10
oil can 56
onion 35
orange (color) 12
orange (fruit) 34
out and about 58–59
oval 10
oven 33
owl 4

P

paint 27
paint box 12
paintbrush 56
painting 28
pajamas 17, 23
pancake 25
panda 46
parrot 37
party 42–43
party hat 42
patterns 11
peach 34
pear 34
pen 13
pencils 27
penguin 46
pentagon 10
pepper 35
pets 37
phone 18
phone booth 30
piano 44
pig 40
piglet 36
pillows 23
pineapple 34
pink 13
pinwheel 38
pitcher 32
pizza 25
plaid 11
plane (airplane) 48
plane (tool) 56
plates 33
playtime 62
pliers 56

plowing a field 40
polar bear 4, 46
pole 31
police 30
pony 40
potatoes 35
presents 43
protractor 27
pruner 56
puppet 28
puppy 36
purple 13

Q

quilt 23

R

rabbit 37
radio 19
radishes 35
raft 48
rainbow 60
raincoat 60
rake 20
rear window 14
recorder 44
rectangle 10
recycling bin 30
red 12, 13
refrigerator 32
reindeer 46
rhino 47
ribbons 42
rice 24
right triangle 10
river 58
robot 28
robot car 29
rocket 52
roof (car) 14
roof (house) 19
rooster 41
rose 20
rubber boots 20
rug 18
ruler 27

S

salad 25
sandwiches 42
saucepan 32
saw 57
saxophone 44
school 27, 62
school uniform 17
scissors 27
scooter 49
scorpion 51
scrambled eggs 25
screwdriver 56
sea 38–39
seafood 25
seal 47
seashell 1
seasons 61
shampoo 22
shapes 10
shark 46
shears 20
sheep 41
shell 39
shirt 5, 17
shoes 4, 17
shopping 54–55
shorts 17
shoulder 2
shovel 38
side-view mirror 15
sidewalk 31
silver 12
sister 26
skateboard 48
sky 21
sleep 23
sleepover 23
slippers 17, 23
slug 51
snail 51
snake 47
sneakers 17
snow 60
snowmobile 48
soap 22
socks 17
sofa 18

son 26
space shuttle 49
speed camera 30
sphere 10
spider 50
spots 11
spring 61
square 10
stars 10, 11
statue 30
steak 25
steamroller 1, 52
steering wheel 15
strawberries 25, 34
streetcar 49
street lamp 30, 31
string beans 35,
stripes 11
stuffed animals 29
summer 61
sun 22
sunglasses 39
surfer 39
swan 46
sweatshirt 17
swimming 38

T

tacos 24
taillight 14
tambourine 44
tape measure 56
tarantula 51
tart 43
teacup 33
teapot 32
teddy 23
teeth 16, 22
television 19
thumb 4
tiger 1, 47
time 62
toaster 32
toilet 23
toilet paper 22
tomato 34
toolbox 57
tools 56–57
toothbrush 22, 62

toothpaste 22
tornado 60
tortoise 37
tower 31
toys 28–29
toy store 54
tractor 41
traffic light 30
train 48
train station 59
trash can 30
tree 21, 52
tree house 21
triangle (instrument) 44
triangle (ruler) 27
tricycle 29
trombone 45
trowel 20, 56
truck 49

tummy 16
turkey (bird) 40
turkey (food) 25
turnip 35

U

umbrella 60

V

vegetables 35
vehicles 48–49
viola 45
violin 44
vise 57

W

wading 38
wake-up time 62
wall 19
washcloth 22
washing the dog 37
washing machine 32
wasps 51
watercraft 48

waterfall 58
watering can 20
watermelon 34
waves 38
wavy 11
weather 60
whale 52
wheat 40
wheel 14
wheelbarrow 20
whisk 33
white 13
wild animals 46–47
window 19, 31
windshield 15
winter 61
wolf 46
wooden blocks 28
workshop 56–57
worm 50
wrapping paper 43
wrench 56, 57

Y

yellow 12, 13

Z

zebra 46
zigzag 11

Created, designed, and edited for Salariya by:
Elizabeth Branch
Stephen Haynes
David Stewart
Rob Walker
Mark Williams

For the National Geographic Society
Priyanka Lamichhane, *Project Editor*
Jonathan Halling, *Design Director*
Kathryn Robbins, *Design Production Assistant*
Lori Epstein, *Senior Illustrations Editor*

First published in North America in 2011 by
National Geographic Society
1145 17th Street N.W.
Washington, D.C. 20036-4688

Library of Congress Cataloging-in-Publication Data
Word book: learning the words in your world.
      p. cm.
Includes index.
ISBN 978-1-4263-0789-8 (alk. paper)
ISBN 978-1-4263-0790-4 (library binding : alk. paper)
1. Vocabulary. I. National Geographic Society (U.S.)
PE1449.W623 2011
428.1--dc22
                                    2010049462

Photo credits: Banana Stock Ltd, Brand X Pictures, Corbis, Digital Stock Corporation, Digital Vision, Ingram Publishing, iStockphoto, John Foxx Images, Jonathan Salariya, Shutterstock, Photodisc, Power Photos

Printed in China
11/SAL/1

Printed on paper from sustainable sources.

PAPER FROM
SUSTAINABLE
FORESTS

Answer to question on page 5: 72 bears